Lester the Library Dog

Dedicated to librarians.

May there always be libraries full of books on shelves with real pages to turn, and cosy reading nooks.

Dedicated also to the wonderful library dogs who inspire children to read, and who make such a difference in their communities.

Gina Dawson

Lester

THE LIBRARY DOG

Gina Dawson

Illustrated by
Bima Perera

NH
NEW
HOLLAND

Lester loves lots of things. He loves games, walks, children, grown-ups, cuddles, snoozing, tummy rubs, stories, Lara, and, of course, the library! Lara is a school librarian and Lester is a library dog.

It's Tuesday, and Tuesday means library day for Lester. Lester's tail goes thump, thump as Lara gets ready. She puts on her badge and fetches Lester's bandana.

At school everyone is pleased to see Lester. Lester's tail wags as he greets his friends. Every few steps there's a new friend to greet.

Lara looks at her watch. "Lester, everyone loves you, and you love everyone, but I need to get to the library!" she laughs. She scoops up Lester and hurries him past his friends.

In the library, Lara prepares for the day, while Lester investigates new smells that have appeared since his last visit. He wags his tail as people pop their heads around the door to say hello.

A boy comes in.

"Today is Jack's first day at this school," his teacher says. "He feels upset and scared and wants to go home."

Lester stops exploring and hurries towards Jack.

Snuggling in, Lester listens as Jack tells him about moving house. As Jack talks, he becomes calmer, and when the bell rings he says, "I'll come back later, Lester," and goes with the teacher to his classroom.

A class arrives. Lara checks Lester's story roster.

"Sally," she says, "have you chosen a book to read to Lester?"

"Yes," says Sally, heading for Lester and the reading nook. Sally reads and Lester listens carefully. When she finishes, Lester's tail goes thump, thump.

"Good work, Sally," says Lara. "Now it's Ramon's turn."

Ramon hurries over to read to Lester. He used to read slowly with a big frown, and sometimes he wouldn't read at all. Now Ramon loves reading! He reads to Lester with a smile, pointing to pictures as he goes.

"Great reading, Ramon!" says Lara.

Lester's morning goes quickly. He listens
to stories and enjoys cuddles.

At lunchtime,
Jacob arrives.

Thump, thump, goes Lester's tail. It's time to head outside for
a lunchtime adventure!

Lester explores the playground, nose twitching. He watches
skipping, joins in a ball game and soaks up the sunshine.
So many smells and things to do! What fun the playground is!

A girl approaches Jacob.

"When I'm bigger I'm going to be a Lester helper," she says.

When lunch ends, Jacob takes a puffed-out Lester to the library. He fills Lester's water bowl and tidies his bed. Then he brushes Lester's coat until it shines.

Lester climbs into his shelf bed and is soon fast asleep.
When the next class arrives, Lester's loud snores have
everyone giggling.

Alice wants to pat Lester, so Lara explains quietly, "Alice, when Lester is in his shelf bed, we let him rest. Lester loves books and children, but sometimes he needs time for himself."

Alice nods.

"Lester's shelf bed is his very own space,
where no-one bothers him."

"How long will Lester be in bed?" Alice asks.

"That's up to Lester," says Lara.

Alice is disappointed.

Lara says, "Lester looks after us, and we look after Lester. When Lester is ready, he will come down and join the class again."

Soon the snoring stops, and the children watch hopefully. Lester stretches, shakes and hops out of bed, ready to mingle again.

The next class is for the littlest children.
Mia and Zoe squabble over a book.

Lester hurries over.

He pushes his way between the girls and rolls over, waiting for a tummy rub. The girls laugh, rub Lester's tummy, and forget their quarrel. When the lesson ends, they leave the library the best of friends.

The final class for the day arrives. Ethan feels angry. He bangs his books down with a thud, can't sit still and isn't listening.

He feels something nudging his leg.

Ethan looks down and sees Lester's worried face. He reaches for Lester and strokes his soft fur. By the end of the lesson, Ethan's anger has faded away. "Thanks, Lester," he says, and he leaves the library quietly.

At home time, Nadia appears. Nadia was once afraid of dogs and stayed away. Now she visits Lester often.

"It's amazing," says Nadia's dad.

"Lester loves children, and most children love Lester," Lara says. "He's a perfect listener and cuddler!"

Lester's tail goes thump, thump.

Lara gathers her things, and she and Lester head home, happy with their day's work.

Lester has helped children who are afraid, angry and sad to feel better. He's listened to stories and had lots of cuddles. He's had fun in the playground and seen his friends. Lester is a tired but happy dog.

That night, Lara and Lester snuggle down to sleep,
and Lester can't wait to do it all again on Friday.

Gina Dawson is the author of several children's books about dogs with jobs. She has also authored books about a variety of social issues for young readers.

Before retiring to write, Gina was an educator and counsellor, presenting programs on a variety of social issues in schools. She is a lifelong lover of dogs, a volunteer to an assistance dog organisation, and an experienced trainer.

When she is not researching, writing or dreaming up new ideas, Gina ghost writes memoirs for adults, along with the occasional short story. Outside of writing she has a diverse range of interests and a long bucket list. She lives with her husband Jim and their dynamic dog, Kiera.

Lester the Library Dog and *Reggie the Rescue Dog* are her twelfth and thirteenth books.

More about Gina's work can be found at www.ginadawson.com.

Bima Perera is an Australian illustrator residing in the bustling city of Tokyo. Born in Japan to Sri Lankan parents and raised in Brisbane, she grew up across multiple cultural settings, where language sometimes became a barrier. This experience enhanced her ability to communicate visually through her drawings.

Bima primarily works with gouache paint. She loves the warmth and nostalgia of the traditional medium, and hopes her illustrations will bring you back to those cosy feelings from your childhood days.

When she isn't painting, she enjoys cooking and illustrating her recipes, holding art classes for kids, and exploring the Japanese countryside with her husband and their adorable rescue dog, Billie.

You can see more of her work at www.bimaillustration.com.

Other recent working dog titles by Gina Dawson

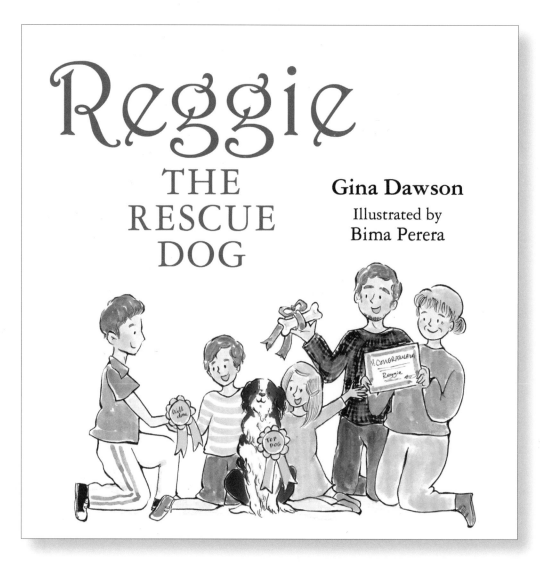

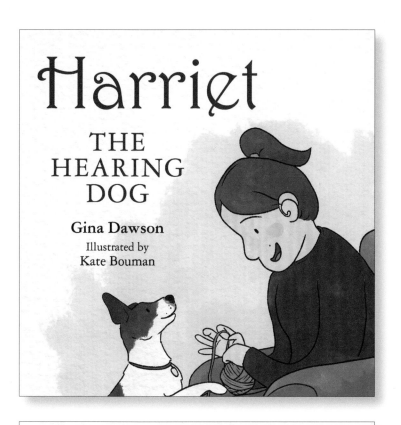

Harriet
THE HEARING DOG

Gina Dawson

Illustrated by
Kate Bouman

Gus
THE GUIDE DOG

Gina Dawson

Illustrated by
Kate Bouman

STOP - 118

First published in 2023 by New Holland Publishers
Sydney • Auckland

Level 1, 178 Fox Valley Road, Wahroonga, NSW 2076, Australia

newhollandpublishers.com

A record of this book is held at the National Library of Australia.

ISBN 9781760795238

Group Managing Director: Fiona Schultz
Project Editor: Liz Hardy
Designer: Andrew Davies
Production Director: Arlene Gippert
Printed in China

10 9 8 7 6 5 4 3 2 1

Keep up with New Holland Publishers:

f NewHollandPublishers

⌾ @newhollandpublishers